SECRET SPACES
IMAGINARY PLACES

Creating Your Own Worlds for Play

Elin McCoy

illustrations by Lynn Sweat

Macmillan Publishing Company   New York

For
Gavin McCoy Walker,
my favorite builder
of spaces and places

—E.M.

Acknowledgments

Many thanks to all the kids and grown-ups who tried the projects that ended up in this book, especially Gavin McCoy Walker, Martha Norman, Bianca Posner and the kids in Corlears School's summer camp program, and John F. Walker. And thanks to Phil Warner of the Cornell University Cooperative Extension for his useful information on treehouse building.

Macmillan Publishing Company, 866 Third Avenue, New York, NY 10022
Collier Macmillan Canada, Inc.

Printed in the United States of America   10 9 8 7 6 5 4 3 2 1

The text of this book is set in 12 pt. Quorum.
The illustrations are rendered in pen-and-ink.
Library of Congress Cataloging-in-Publication Data
McCoy, Elin. Secret spaces, imaginary places.
Summary: Provides instructions for constructing a variety of play spaces including pirate ships, castles, Indian teepees, and secret hideouts using inexpensive and free materials.   1. Playhouses, Children's—Juvenile literature.   2. Handicraft—Juvenile literature.   [1. Building. 2. Handicraft] I. Sweat, Lynn, ill. II. Title.
TH4967.M38 1986   745.592   85-23089   ISBN 0-02-765460-5

Contents

Note to Kids Using This Book

No matter where you live, you need a private place or secret space that's just for you. Building one is what this book is all about. I built a lot of these places when I was your age, and now my son, nieces, nephews, and other children I know are building them. You can too—in your room, a basement, a garage, or backyard.

Some of these places do require an outdoor space. If you have only a small yard or live in an apartment with no yard at all, don't give up. There may be a vacant lot nearby that you could use. You may be able to use an area of a park or playground. But it is important to get permission first.

Before you start any project in this book, read over the instructions and check on the materials and tools you'll need. Some projects are much easier than others and will take very little time to complete. Others are long projects that require adult help.

One last thought: I hope you have fun! Let me know what you like and what you don't.

Safety Rules

The three basic rules:

1. If you've never used a particular tool, get an adult to show you how before you use it.

2. Always ask an adult before you use a sharp knife or saw, make a fire, or handle sharp materials.

3. Always ask an adult to check that any structure you have built is safe.

Here are some others:

- Wear work gloves when you handle any sharp materials or collect junk materials.
- Use tools carefully. Work slowly. That's better than getting hurt.
- Never play with tools. Use them only as you are supposed to use them.
- Take care of your tools. Dull blades can be dangerous.
- Never leave nails around and never leave wood around that has nails sticking out of it.
- Don't use superglues that can make your fingers stick together.
- Keep an emergency kit full of Band-Aids, first-aid cream, and antiseptic wipes handy.

Materials and Where to Get Them

You can find most of the materials needed to build the spaces and places in this book around your house or for free from places nearby. Keep collecting and saving interesting household items your parents or neighbors throw away and check regularly with grocery stores and shops.

Things at Home

At home, here are the kinds of things you should look for:

old sheets and blankets
cardboard tubes and boxes
old shower curtains
fabric scraps
scrap wood and plywood
old broomsticks and mop handles
metal shower-curtain rings
clothesline
rope
twine
string
flashlights
plastic milk jugs
big pieces of plastic that come
  wrapped around new furniture
rocks and stones
old bricks
tent stakes
clothespins
safety pins
rubber bands
paint

Free Items

In your community, there are many ways to get interesting, useful items for free. If you live in a city, call the sanitation department to find out when they pick up big objects in your neighborhood. This will let you know when people will be putting out items for collection.

You can get big cardboard cartons—the kind refrigerators and other appliances come in—from appliance stores and department stores. Ask them to save you one or two. Also check in your neighborhood. Someone may have just bought a refrigerator and thrown away the carton.

Go with a parent or other grown-up to your local dump. You may be able to salvage items such as old furniture, wooden telephone-wire spools, concrete blocks, tires and inner tubes, crates, old mattress springs.

Things to Buy

Here is a list of things you may have to buy and where to get them.

wood Buy it at a lumber store. The store will cut it to size for you if you want. Plywood is made of layers of wood pressed together. Exterior plywood is for outdoor projects. All plywood comes in 4-foot by 8-foot sheets and different thicknesses. Sometimes lumber stores have scrap lumber they give away.

nails Buy them at a lumber store or hardware store. They come in different sizes. The right-size nail for a project is one that is long enough to go through one board and at least a $1/2$ inch into the board you're joining it to.

duct tape This is heavy, reinforced tape that you can buy at hardware stores. It is much, much stronger than masking tape or Scotch tape.

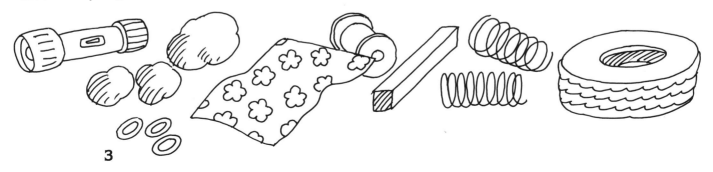

Basic Tools and Supplies and How to Use Them

You'll need some basic tools to build many of the spaces and places in this book. The directions for each project will tell you which ones to use. Your parents will probably have most of these tools and supplies somewhere around the house. In fact, the only one you are likely to have to buy is a mat knife, but all these common tools and supplies can be purchased at a hardware store if necessary. Always ask permission before you borrow any tool.

tape measure

yardstick

steel ruler

hammer

pliers

saw

mat knife (also called utility knife)
This knife is the best tool for cutting cardboard. It has a replaceable blade and is available in hardware and art supply stores.

hatchet or ax

bread knife

scissors

C-clamp or vise

screwdriver

level

sandpaper

white glue, such as Elmer's

stapler

pencils and felt-tip pens

paint and paint roller

Keep the tools you need for each project in a cardboard box. But if you don't finish the project right away, remember to return the tools and supplies to their place in case someone else needs them before you're ready to start work again.

Paint

Water-based latex house paint works best on cardboard and wood. You can wash your hands and brushes in just soapy water. Spills are easy to mop up with a sponge and water. A roller (not a paintbrush) is the easiest way to paint cardboard. Don't make paint on cardboard too thick or the cardboard will warp.

How to Use a Saw

Your saw should be sharp. A dull one is dangerous. Lay the wood you want to saw on a workbench or solid surface. Draw a line where you want to cut. Hold the wood steady and in place with a vise or C-clamp. This is very important. Make sure the part you want to cut is about an inch out from the surface of the workbench. Try to use even, steady, long strokes as you saw on the line. You can cut cardboard with a saw too.

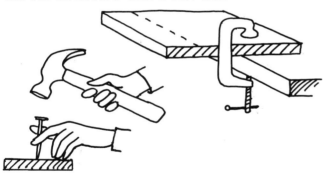

How to Hammer in a Nail

Hold the nail between your thumb and first finger and tap a few times squarely on the nail's head until it takes hold. Then hammer the nail harder. Hammer nails in straight.

How to Cut Cardboard

The best way to cut cardboard is with a steel ruler and a mat knife. You can buy mat knives at hardware and art-supply stores. Draw straight lines where you want to cut and lay the carton down. Put a piece of masonite or scrap lumber underneath before you begin to cut. Put the steel ruler against the line and press the knife blade into the cardboard along the side of the ruler. Work slowly. Keep the hand holding the knife above the blade and your other hand parallel with the ruler so you can't cut your fingers. The blade on this knife is very sharp. You might need to press the blade along the line several times before you've cut through the cardboard completely. (You can also cut cardboard with a saw or bread knife, but unless the blade is very sharp it shreds the cardboard and leaves a rough edge.)

To score cardboard means to cut only partway through it so it will fold easily and neatly along the scored line.

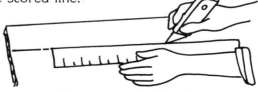

How to Cut Cardboard

Three Basic Knots

For some of the projects in this book (mostly tents), you'll need to know how to tie a few basic knots. The simple knot, the square knot, and the half-hitch are all easy to tie. But it helps if you practice tying them a few times <u>before</u> you start your project. All you need is a piece of rope.

Simple Knot

1. Make a loop like this. Put one end of a rope over the other.

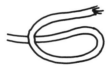

2. Now bring the end of the rope back through the loop like this.

3. Pull both ends to tighten.

Square Knot

1. Cross two ends of rope. Put the end in your right hand on top of the end in your left hand.

2. Bring it under and up, like this.

3. Cross the two ends of rope again. Be sure to put the end that's in your left hand now over the one that's in your right hand.

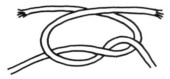

4. Bring it under and up. Your knot should look like this. Pull the ends away from each other to tighten the knot.

Two Half-Hitches

1. Wrap one end of the rope around a tree twice. Pull tight.

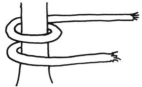

2. Loop the short end under and over the other part of the rope, like this.

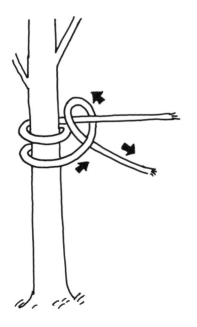

3. Pull it down toward the tree to make it as tight as you can. Now you've done one half-hitch.

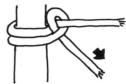

4. One half-hitch usually won't hold, so you need another. Make it exactly the same way, using the short end of the rope again. Pull it down and in tight.

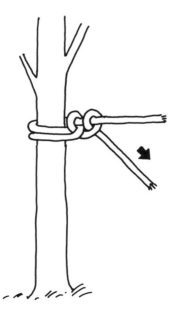

Imaginary Places

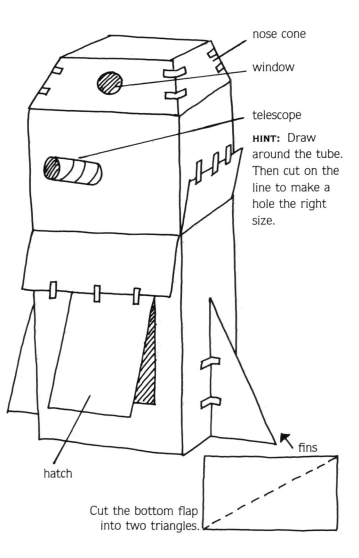

nose cone

window

telescope

HINT: Draw around the tube. Then cut on the line to make a hole the right size.

Spaceship

A lot of kids like to imagine what it would be like to travel to outer space. Do you? You'll be all ready to take off on an imaginary adventure with this super interplanetary spaceship made from two big cardboard boxes, the kind stoves or dishwashers come in. Here's a list of supplies:

> 2 big cardboard boxes with top and
>   bottom flaps open
> 1 paper-towel tube
> silver duct tape
> mat knife or other sharp knife
> steel ruler
> felt-tip markers
> paintbrush
> water-based white or gray latex paint

Here's the spaceship plan. Add your own ideas.

hatch

fins

Cut the bottom flap into two triangles.

Cut a bottom flap from one box. The easiest way is to use a mat knife. Read how to cut cardboard on page 5 before you use the knife. Stand the box so the end with all four flaps is at the top. Cut two triangle shapes from the cut-off bottom flap to make the fins. Tape them to opposite sides of the box.

Trim the corners off the top flaps of the other box. Pull them up and tape them together to form the nose cone.

Set the nose cone box on top of the standing box. Pull out two opposite flaps of the standing box and tape them to the <u>outside</u> of the nose cone box. Tape the other two opposite flaps <u>inside</u> the nose cone box. Tape the bottom flaps of the nose cone box in the same way.

Draw a square big enough for you to crawl through on one side of the standing box. Cut along the side and bottom lines to make a flap. That's your entrance hatch.

Draw and cut out a circle on the other side to make a window. Cut several small circles of different sizes in the nose cone box. One should be the same size as a paper-towel tube. Slide in the tube and tape it in place. That's your telescope.

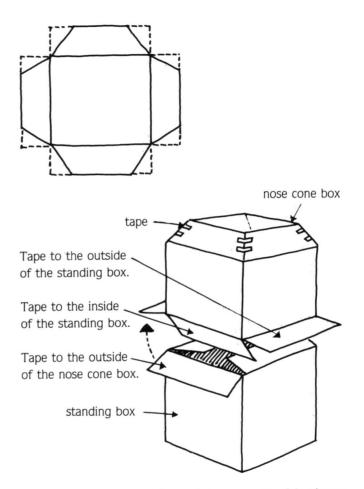

nose cone box

tape

Tape to the outside of the standing box.

Tape to the inside of the standing box.

Tape to the outside of the nose cone box.

standing box

Paint your spaceship and decorate it with pieces of silver duct tape.

controls

LOG

Now for your equipment. First, make the control panel. Draw dials and screens on one of the inside flaps with colored markers. Glue on buttons, bottle caps, corks, and spools for knobs and buttons to push. Tape the panel at an angle inside the spaceship.

Add an inner-tube seat (to absorb gravity forces) and take along flashlights for laser cannons, a walkie-talkie, and earphones. To make a pretend walkie-talkie, draw buttons on a small box and tape on a straw for an aerial.

Don't forget to keep a spaceship log to record your route, what's on the planets you visit, and the alien beings you encounter.

Cardboard Castle

You'll need a lot of cardboard to build this castle, so start collecting boxes, flat sheets, and tubes of all sizes right away. It won't take long to find enough if you ask at supermarkets and other stores near your home for the boxes they throw away.

When you have all your cardboard, gather your tools and other supplies—wide silver duct tape, a mat knife or other sharp knife, a ball of heavy twine, a steel ruler, a screwdriver, and a pencil. Read how to cut cardboard (page 5) before you begin.

Some boxes will have flaps at opposite ends. Open those flaps. Flaps make it easy to join boxes together to make a castle. Slide opposite side flaps of two boxes into each other like this and tape the flaps on the inside and the outside.

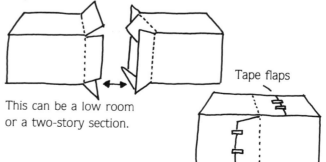

Tape flaps

This can be a low room or a two-story section.

You can also use boxes that don't have flaps. As you cut connecting passageways, you'll create flaps. Here's how to join a smaller box to a bigger one.

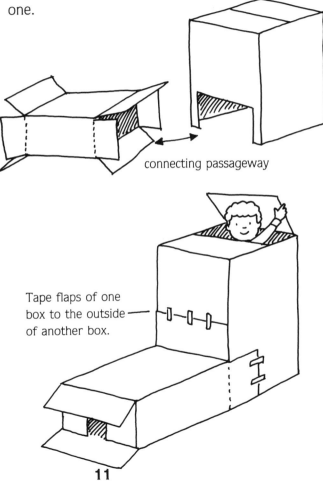

connecting passageway

Tape flaps of one box to the outside of another box.

11

Keep joining boxes until your castle is the size you want. Put in plenty of lookout slots and spyholes, make a tunnel to a secret room, attach towers and flags, and don't forget to include a big box with a drawbridge entrance in it. Here's how to make one.

Draw a rectangle on the front of the box and cut on three sides like the one in the picture. Make a hole with a screwdriver in each top corner of the drawbridge and a matching one just above it in the box wall. Cut two pieces of twine about 4 feet long. Tie a square knot (see page 6) in one end of each. Thread each piece of twine through one drawbridge hole with the knot on the outside. Then pull it through the hole in the box and tie square knots in the ends. Pull to raise the drawbridge; push to lower it.

This is what your cardboard castle might look like.

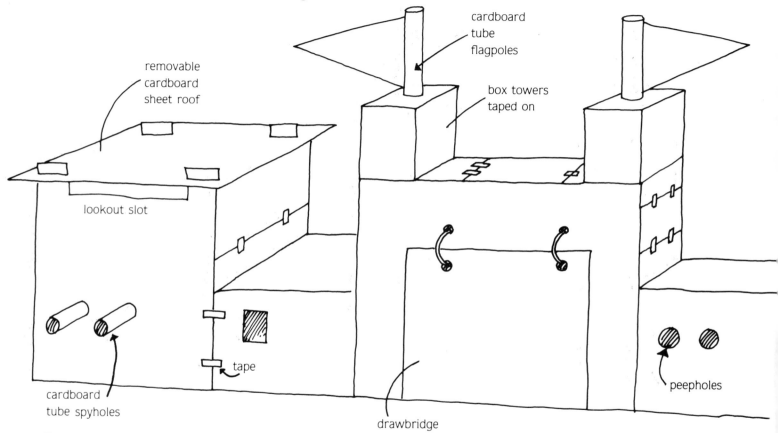

removable cardboard sheet roof

cardboard tube flagpoles

box towers taped on

lookout slot

tape

cardboard tube spyholes

drawbridge

peepholes

Draw around the tube. Cut out the circle with a mat knife. Push in the tube and tape it.

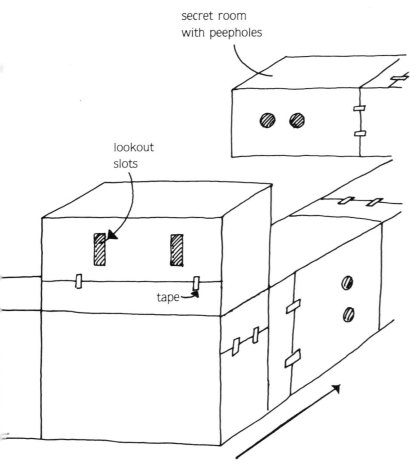

secret room
with peepholes

lookout
slots

tape

Make a long tunnel to a secret room.
Tape together boxes that are the same size.
Join them to another bigger box that has peepholes.

What to Do in Your Castle

Be knights. They lived in castles long ago, during the Middle Ages. Here's what you need.

Sword

Draw a sword shape like this one on a cardboard sheet. Make it about 1½ feet long. After you cut it out, trace around it on another piece of cardboard and cut that out. Tape the two pieces back to back with silver duct tape. If you want to, you can put silver tape on the blade and paint a small design on the handle to match your shield.

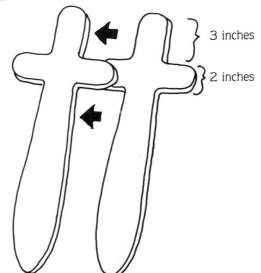

3 inches

2 inches

Shield

Cut out two matching shield shapes (like these) from cardboard sheets. Make them about 1½ feet wide and 2 feet long. Poke two sets of holes in the center of one shape. Make the sets about 1 inch apart. Make the top holes about 4 inches above the bottom ones. Thread a piece of heavy twine 1 foot long through each hole. (Make loops on one side <u>just</u> big enough for your hand.) Tie the ends together to make the shield handle. Use a square knot (see page 6). Cut off extra twine.

Put the shields back to back and tape the edges together. Paint your shield the way real knights did. A cross or stripes or a chevron is easy; a dragon is harder, but looks great.

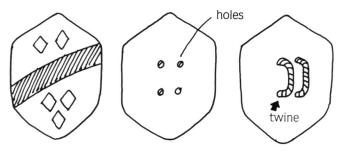

holes

twine

HINT: Paint the background first. When it's dry, paint on the design.

Helmet

Find a small box that fits on your head. Cut off the bottom panels and most of the front one. Cut a visor shape from the big panel. It will go across the front of the helmet. Poke two holes in each side of the visor and two matching holes in each side of the helmet. Roll up the visor so it is curved. Attach it to the helmet by threading a 6-inch piece of twine through the holes in each side of the visor and helmet and tying it with a square knot (see page 6). Tape feathers or curled paper on top for a plume.

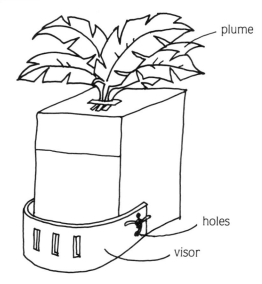

plume

holes

visor

14

Pirate Ship

On a rainy afternoon when you can't go anywhere without getting wet, you can go hunting for treasure inside in this cardboard pirate ship—if you are smart enough to keep a big cardboard box on hand. The kind of box that a refrigerator or a big piece of furniture comes in is perfect.

Do you have your box? Get your cardboard-cutting tools ready: a mat knife or other strong knife, a steel ruler, and a pencil. Read about how to cut cardboard on page 5 before you start.

You might as well get out the rest of the things you'll need: a roll of strong silver duct tape, some pieces of scrap cardboard, an old broomstick or mop handle, scissors, a discarded white sheet, cardboard tubes, felt-tip markers, and paint and paintbrushes.

Lay your box down on its side, with the flaps open at one end. With your mat knife cut off the top and bottom flaps from the open end. Attach them to the ends of the remaining (side) flaps with tape. Bring the two long flaps together and tape them to make the bow.

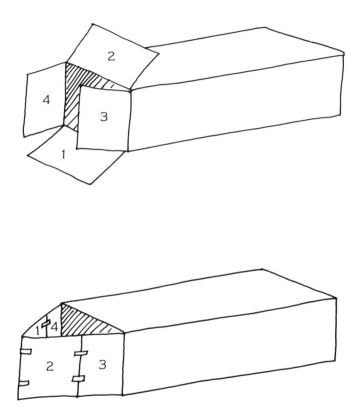

Cut a rectangle in the center of the box, part way down the sides. Cut a small hole into the rear deck of the boat for the mast. Push in the broomstick and anchor it at the bottom of the boat with duct tape.

Paint the boat. While it's drying, make the sail and the flag plus your pirate outfit.

For the sail, cut a 3-foot-square piece from the old sheet. Staple it to two heavy strips of cardboard. Tape the center of one cardboard strip to the top of the mast and the other lower down on the mast.

For a skull and crossbones flag, cut a triangle from the sheet. Draw a skull and crossbones on it with a black felt marker. Tape the flag to the mast.

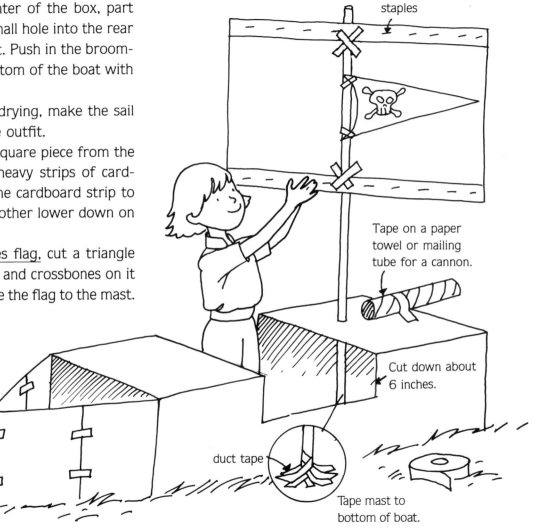

staples

Tape on a paper towel or mailing tube for a cannon.

Cut down about 6 inches.

duct tape

Tape mast to bottom of boat.

Here's Your Pirate Costume

Pirate captains wore hats like this. Cut two pieces of cardboard this shape. Draw a skull and cross-bones on one. Staple them together at each end.

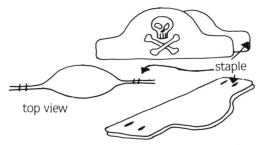

top view

staple

To make your eyepatch, cut a small oval of black cloth or paper and staple the end of a piece of elastic (your mother may have some in a sewing box) to each side.

Pirates carried swords called cutlasses and knives called daggers. They also carried pistols. Make them all from scrap pieces of cardboard.

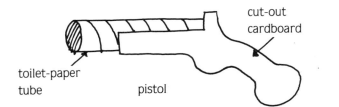

cut-out cardboard

toilet-paper tube

pistol

P.S. Don't forget a treasure map. X marks the spot where the treasure is hidden. Fill a small box with jewelry and play money (see page 73).

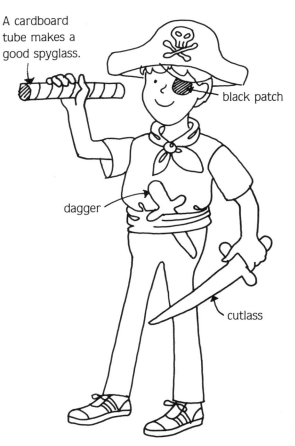

A cardboard tube makes a good spyglass.

black patch

dagger

cutlass

17

Creepy Halloween Tunnel

A dark, creepy tunnel full of weird, scary surprises is just the thing for your next Halloween party. A dark basement or garage is an ideal place to set it up, but a large room in a house or apartment will do. Or you can put it outdoors.

Here are two ways to make a tunnel—you'll probably be able to think of many more. No matter how you build it, remember that your tunnel should be tall enough for kids to walk through and dark enough so they'll be scared by all the creepy stuff you've put in it. It shouldn't be so dark no one can see anything at all.

Cardboard Box Tunnel

Collect at least six big cardboard boxes—the kind refrigerators come in, or even bigger. It doesn't matter if they're not all the same size. Line them up the way you want them for your tunnel. Cut out the sides where they touch. Connect them to one another with heavy reinforced tape.

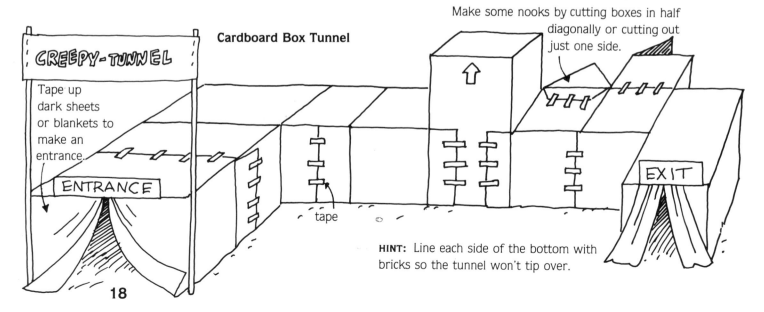

Cardboard Box Tunnel

CREEPY-TUNNEL

Tape up dark sheets or blankets to make an entrance.

ENTRANCE

tape

Make some nooks by cutting boxes in half diagonally or cutting out just one side.

EXIT

HINT: Line each side of the bottom with bricks so the tunnel won't tip over.

18

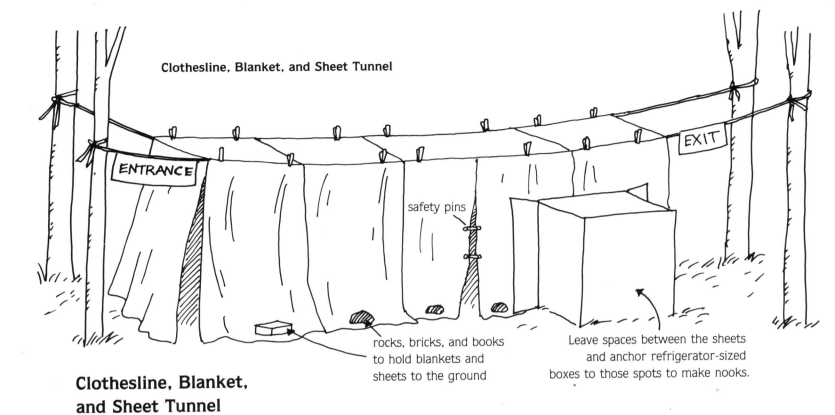

Clothesline, Blanket, and Sheet Tunnel

ENTRANCE

EXIT

safety pins

rocks, bricks, and books
to hold blankets and
sheets to the ground

Leave spaces between the sheets
and anchor refrigerator-sized
boxes to those spots to make nooks.

Clothesline, Blanket, and Sheet Tunnel

Put up two clotheslines about 5 feet high and about 4 or 5 feet apart. Running them from one door to another works the very best because you can use the doors as your entrance and exit. But two parallel clotheslines outdoors will work pretty well, too. Tie the clotheslines to something that won't fall down—a door hinge, a heavy hook, a tree if you're making your tunnel outside. Tie short pieces of clothesline or twine across the two clotheslines so you'll have a way to hang creepy things. Clip dark-colored sheets and blankets to the clotheslines to make the tunnel sides and the entrance and exit. Drape more across the top.

P.S. Remember the idea is only to scare kids, not hurt them. Make sure your tunnel has no sharp nails or splintery wood, nothing to cause people to trip and fall, and nothing to ruin kids' clothes. Most of all, remember that really little kids are easily scared. Use the tunnel for kids your own age.

Fill your tunnel with lots of creepy, spooky, sinister, weird, scary things.

To See

Hang these from the ceiling of your tunnel:

- a rubber glove filled with water and tied at the top (Pierce the fingertips with a pin if your tunnel is outdoors.)
- spiders made from black yarn or pipe cleaners
- spider webs made from white thread or yarn
- papier-mâché skulls (Mold papier-mâché around a balloon to look like a skull—see page 71 for how to make papier-mâché. When it's dry, pop the balloon.)
- bats made from pieces of old inner tube
- a cardboard skeleton
- scary masks
- long strips of wet cloth (only if your tunnel is outdoors)

Add:

- a friend dressed in black and wearing a Frankenstein mask hiding in a nook, who makes weird moaning sounds as kids come through
- a long sausage-shaped balloon filled with helium and covered with a white scarf—it will float around and look like a ghost
- flashlights with red or green cellophane taped over the light
- and anything else you can think of that would look scary

To Hear

Play a tape recording of creepy sound effects:

- cats yowling
- something metal being pulled across cement
- dull thuds (Wrap heavy books or rocks in a blanket and drop them on something metal.)
- clanking and rattling chains
- high-pitched screeches and bloodcurdling screams (Don't use these too much.)
- heavy breathing
- cackling witch's laugh
- feet in heavy boots walking up the stairs, coming closer and closer

P.S. Ordinary noises will sound weird if you record them at fast or slow speeds instead of normal.

21

To Feel

For an even more spooky time, hold out bowls and buckets of yucky objects kids have to touch as they walk through.

- wet noodles (Tell kids these are intestines or worms.)
- peeled grapes (eyeballs)
- cauliflower coated with vegetable oil (someone's brain)
- a canned tomato (heart)
- large washed but wet chicken bones (skeleton)
- rubber spiders

Some more ideas: Tickle the person with a feather or piece of dried grass and say it's a spider or a bat. Tap your friend's arms with long, pointed fingernails (tape them on) and say it's a witch's hand. Set up a dust mop feelie like this:

Tents, Tarps, and Teepees

The Arab Sheik's Tent

It takes only five minutes to put up this tent and you can set it up indoors or outdoors. It's the perfect tent for kids who live in apartments and the best tent for a bedroom. You may even want to leave it up for a while so you'll have a place to get away from it all.

Drape two old twin-bed-sized sheets or blankets over a card table, overlapping them on top. Put something heavy on the overlap to hold them in place. Pin one flap up to make a doorway.

P.S. This tent is also good for lounging around and reading books in private. (You'll need a flashlight or a lamp.) You can even sleep in it—if you can curl up enough to fit.

Sheik's Tent

What to Do in Your Tent

Be an Arab sheik. Cover the floor of your tent with a colorful rug and then line it with pillows and cushions the way Bedouins in Arab countries do. Make a sheik-style robe and headgear from a discarded white sheet and pillowcase, colored belts or the tie from a bathrobe, and a sweatband.

If you don't have a card table, drape your sheets over four chairs and pin them together, like this:

pillowcase

sweatband

sheet with hole
for neck as robe

belt

Wear sandals.

Two More Instant Tents

Get some blankets or sheets and look around your house (or a friend's) for a place you can use as the frame for a tent. Here are two ideas to get you started.

The Porch Railing Tarp Tent

The main thing you need for this tent is a porch with a railing to use as the frame. You'll also need a sheet or blanket that's at least twin-bed-sized, five large safety pins, and some large rocks. Hang one end of the sheet or blanket (the long side works best) over the railing and pin it in place between the posts. Stretch it taut and anchor the opposite side with rocks.

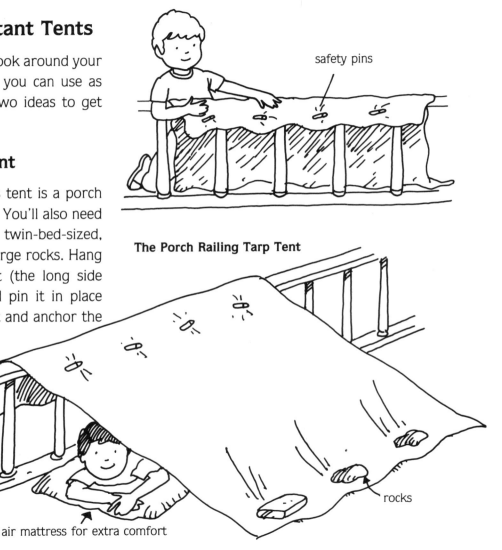

safety pins

The Porch Railing Tarp Tent

air mattress for extra comfort

rocks

24

The Four-Poster Bed Tent

A four-poster bed makes a terrific tent frame. The size and number of sheets you'll need for this tent depends on the size of your four-poster and whether or not it has a canopy. You'll also need very large, strong rubber bands and a few large safety pins.

If your bed is twin-sized

Drape an old king-sized sheet (or overlap two twin-sized sheets) over the four bedposts. Pull the sheet tight as you slide a rubber band over the top of each post to hold the sheet in place. If you don't have rubber bands, or if the bed has a high canopy, you can wrap string around each post. Don't forget to make a doorway.

If you have a double bed

Hang twin-sized sheets on the sides, using rubber bands or string to hold them to the posts. Stretch a double-bed fitted sheet across the top and attach it by rubber bands too. Pin the ends of the twin sheets to the double sheet. If your bed has a canopy, just skip putting on a top—naturally.

The Four-Poster Bed Tent

rubber band

safety pins

Can you think of any more places for an instant tent? This is a stairway tent.

The Stairway Tent

Tents for Backyard Camping Expeditions

One of the nicest things to do with a tent is to set up a campsite outdoors and sleep overnight under the stars. These tents are even simpler to put up than a store-bought one. Having a friend with you on your camping expedition will make it twice as easy and twice as much fun.

For all these tents you need a level grassy area (or at least one without any rocks) near one or two trees. If you use waterproof canvas (available at camping stores), an old shower curtain, or the strong heavy-duty plastic or polyethylene sheeting that's used by painters for drop cloths (you can buy it at hardware stores, camping stores, and sometimes plant nurseries) to make your tent, it will keep rain off you unless there's a downpour. If you're not worried about rain, you can use a thin blanket.

Some Hints on Setting Up Camp

- Plan ahead. Make a list of things you need and gather them together. (See pages 31 and 58 for some ideas.) Check the weather forecast before you drag out all your gear.
- Remove any stones and twigs from the campsite you've picked.
- Practice the three essential knots—simple, square, and two half-hitches (shown on pages 6–7)—before putting up your tent.
- For most of these tents you'll need a groundsheet—a piece of plasticized fabric to put on the ground inside the tent so your sleeping bag stays clean and dry. A shower curtain works fine. Anchor it in the corners with rocks.
- These tents are not mosquitoproof. Use insect repellent before crawling into your sleeping bag.
- If you leave your tent up on the lawn for a week or so, be sure to take up the groundsheet from time to time. Otherwise it will kill the grass underneath.

Mountain Climber's Bivouac Tent

This is a one-tree tent. You'll also need a piece of rope about 20 feet long (such as clothesline), a large piece of heavy-duty plastic sheeting or waterproof canvas about 7 feet by 7 feet or a shower curtain, a regular tent stake or cement block, some shower curtain rings (this kind: ⊂▭), and small stones.

Wrap the rope around the tree twice, about 4 or 5 feet off the ground (see page 28). Tie two half-hitches. Then tie several simple knots in the rope, making them about 2 feet apart. Stretch the rope down to the ground so it makes an angle. Hammer a tent stake into the ground at that spot or put a cement block there. Use two half-hitches to tie the rope to the stake or block.

Now fold one corner of the plastic over a small stone. Loop the big end of the shower curtain ring over it and then twist to the small end to hold the stone in place. Throw the plastic sheet over the rope so that the shower curtain hoop is at one of the knots in the rope.

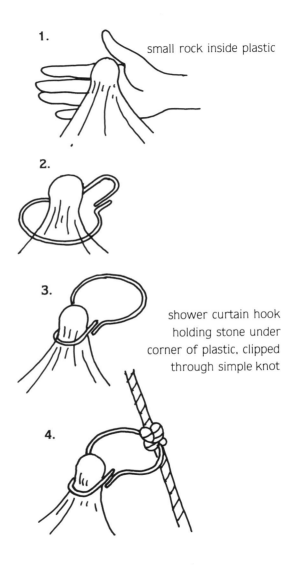

1. small rock inside plastic

2.

3.

shower curtain hook holding stone under corner of plastic, clipped through simple knot

4.

HINT: Before you tighten the second half-hitch, stick a twig in the loop so the knot will be easy to loosen.

Hold the plastic sheet out to make sure the sides of the tent come down far enough to be anchored to the ground. You may have to move the plastic up and down the rope a few times until you find which knot is at the right height. Unclip the shower curtain hook, push it through the knot, and clip it again so the tent is anchored at the knot.

Stretch the sides out, making them as taut as you can. Put four or five rocks or bricks on each side. Put in your groundsheet, and you're all set!

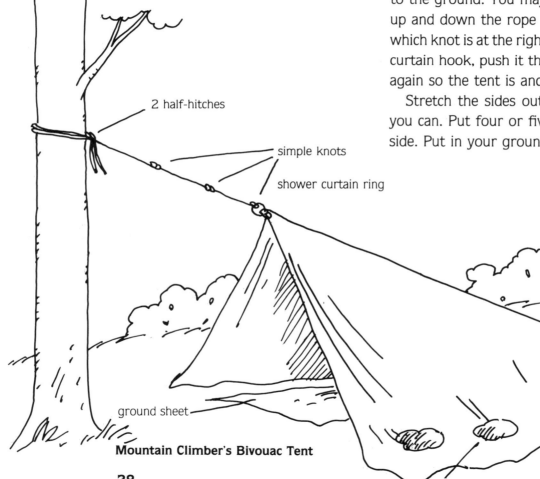

2 half-hitches

simple knots

shower curtain ring

tent stake (or use concrete block)

2 half-hitches

ground sheet

Mountain Climber's Bivouac Tent

rocks

Two-Tree Tents

A-Frame Tent

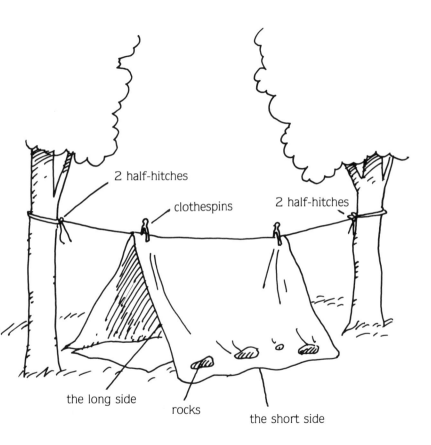

Find two trees that are about 10 feet apart. Get a piece of rope about 20 feet long. Wrap one end twice around one tree, about 3½ to 4 feet off the ground. Tie two half-hitches (see page 7). Wrap the other end twice around the other tree and pull it tight. Tie two more half-hitches.

Now throw a rectangular piece of plastic or a shower curtain over the rope. It should be at least 6 feet by 8 feet so your tent will be at least 3½ feet high and 6 feet long. Fasten the ends of the plastic to the rope with two old-fashioned wooden clothespins, the kind that don't have springs, if you have them. (The tent will work pretty well without them.) Stretch each side out and put three rocks or bricks on each side.

> **P.S.** If you have two smaller pieces of plastic, you can overlap them on the clothesline and clip them with clothespins.

2 half-hitches

clothespins

2 half-hitches

the long side

rocks

the short side

29

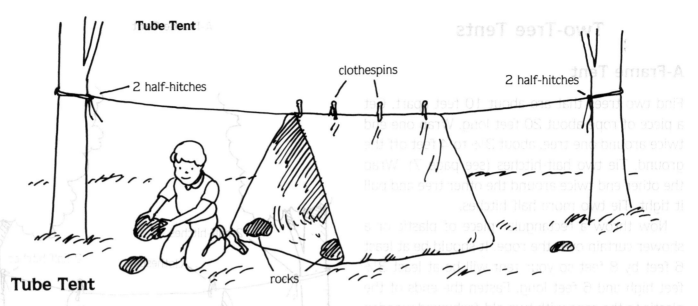

Tube Tent

2 half-hitches

clothespins

2 half-hitches

rocks

Tube Tent

This is another easy two-tree tent. It has a built-in groundsheet. Besides a 20-foot piece of clothesline, you need some rocks, four old-fashioned wooden clothespins (not the kind with springs), and a tube made of polyethylene. You can buy it at a camping store. It won't cost much. Tubes are usually about 3 to 5 feet across and 9 feet long, but some places will cut just the length you want. Sometimes new mattresses and sofas have these tubes around them to protect them. Ask at a local department or furniture store.

Tie one end of the clothesline to one tree about 3½ to 4 feet off the ground. (Wrap it around twice and tie two half-hitch knots.) Then slide the tube along the clothesline and clip it with clothespins. Use the kind that don't have springs. Then wrap the other end of the rope twice around the other tree about the same distance from the ground. Make sure the clothesline is tight before you tie two half-hitches.

Now crawl into the tube and anchor the four corners with rocks.

Essential Provisions for Camping Out in the Backyard

What you'll need will depend on how long an expedition you're planning. Try just an overnight outing first. Here are some supplies to put on your list. Add other items needed for backpacking activities you're interested in—insect-collecting stuff, a bird or tree identification book, sports equipment such as a Frisbee. (The good thing about backyard camping is that you can run home to get whatever you forgot.)

    tent and tent-making equipment
      (see pages 26 to 30)
    extra rope
    flashlight
    jackknife (if you're allowed to use
      knives and know how)
    backpack or rucksack
    sleeping bag or bedroll
    extra clothing (sweatshirt, socks, etc.)
    first-aid kit (Band-Aids, antiseptic
      wipes, first-aid cream)
    insect repellent

food for supper, high-energy snacks, and breakfast (sandwiches, fruit, raisins, nuts, raw vegetables, hard-boiled eggs, cereal and powdered milk, cookies, chocolate, cheese, etc.)
jug or canteen of drinking water; Thermos with cold juice or lemonade or hot cocoa
eating utensils (plastic or paper plates and cups, plastic forks, knives, and spoons)
plastic bag for garbage
air mattress or foam pad to put your sleeping bag on if you want super comfort
Styrofoam chest with ice if you have food that might spoil
binoculars for stargazing and watching birds and animals
a hiking stick
a notebook and pen
matches and cooking gear if you're allowed to make a campfire

How to Make a Bedroll

To make a bedroll, fold two blankets around one another lengthwise, as shown.

Fasten the sides with several large safety pins. Fold up the bottom and pin it too.

Safari Shower

For longer expeditions, set up this safari shower.

Use an ice pick or sharp nail to poke about ten small holes in the bottom of a 1-gallon plastic jug with a handle and a screw-on top. Tie a rope to the handle. Use a square knot (see page 6). Fill the jug to overflowing fast. Screw the top on tight and tie the jug to a tree limb with two half-hitches (see page 7). It won't leak much unless you shake it. Just loosen the top to start the shower. Tighten it to stop. This is great for hot days, sticky hands, and washing fruit and dishes.

2 half-hitches

square knot

holes

Add a soap bar tied to a piece of rope.

What to Do on Your Backyard Camping Expedition

- Plan hiking trips for the daytime. Take your backpack, a trail snack, and your canteen of water. Set up trails in the neighborhood—a piece of colored cloth tied to a tree makes a good trail marker and so does a stack of three rocks.
- Collect plant or animal specimens—leaves, pinecones, insects, whatever you want. Put them in a collecting jar like this one.

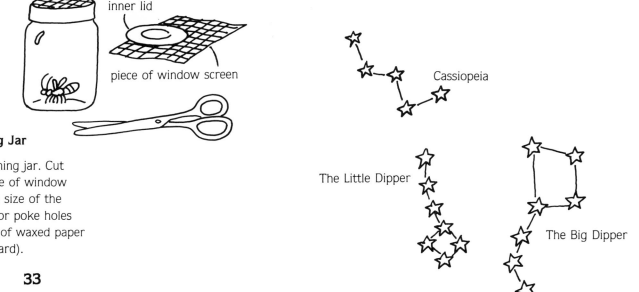

inner lid

piece of window screen

Collecting Jar

Use a canning jar. Cut out a circle of window screen the size of the inner lid (or poke holes in a circle of waxed paper or index card).

- Keep a nature journal. Dawn and dusk are the best times to spot animals and birds. Write down how many different kinds you see. Sketch pictures of trees, plants, and flowers, and find out their names.
- Go on a fishing trip if you have a nearby pond. You can make your own fishing pole—see page 59 for directions.
- At night, sit around the tent telling ghost stories. When they get too scary, sing campfire songs.
- Stargaze. Even if you don't have a telescope or binoculars, you can find these constellations.

Cassiopeia

The Little Dipper

The Big Dipper

An Easy Sioux Indian Teepee

The teepee is a tent that was invented by the Native American tribes who lived on the plains in the Midwest. Each tribe had its own special teepee design.

The American Indians made the frames for their teepees from straight-growing trees such as lodge-pole pine cut into 25-foot-long poles. The frame was covered with buffalo hide, but when the buffalo herds disappeared, the Indians used cowhides and later canvas. All styles of teepees had a smoke-hole at the top and an inner lining to keep the inside as dry as possible. Once the poles were cut and the cover made, a teepee could be set up in twenty minutes.

This small version of a Sioux teepee is about 6 feet high inside and 8 feet across.

You'll need these tools and equipment:

    a good knife

    a hatchet or ax (if you're cutting the poles yourself)

    heavy-duty scissors

    sturdy kitchen stool

    felt pens with permanent ink

You'll need these materials:

    5-foot-long piece of rope

    1 large piece of cloth or plastic 16 feet by at least 8 feet (Use a painter's polyethylene or canvas drop cloth, or heavy-duty tarp fabric from a camping store, or two queen- or king-sized sheets sewn or safety-pinned together on the long side.)

    $8\frac{1}{2}$-foot-long piece of string

    1 pencil or piece of colored chalk

    15 or more rocks

    10 very large safety pins

    9 wooden poles 10 feet long (Cut straight saplings or buy long pieces of bamboo from a nursery. Sharpen one end of each with a knife.)

    1 small rock

    1 shower curtain hoop

To make the teepee cover, lay the cloth out on a flat surface and draw a semicircle on it with chalk. Fasten one end of the string to a stick placed at the center of the long side of the cloth. Fasten the other end to the chalk or pencil. Pull the pencil around so your semicircle has the same diameter all the way around.

Cut out the semicircle. Use felt-tip markers to decorate it. (Felt-tips don't work on some types of plastic.) The designs on real Indian teepees were similar to ones shown here.

When the colors are dry, fold the center of the straight side of the cover around the small rock. Then loop the big end of the shower curtain hoop over it and twist the hoop so the small end is holding the rock in place.

Teepee Designs
Use geometric patterns and animal designs.

safety pins

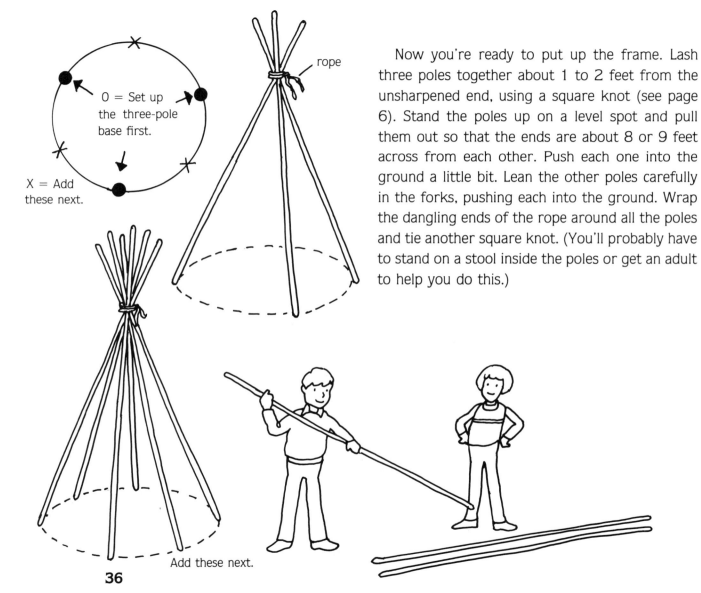

rope

O = Set up
the three-pole
base first.

X = Add
these next.

Add these next.

Now you're ready to put up the frame. Lash three poles together about 1 to 2 feet from the unsharpened end, using a square knot (see page 6). Stand the poles up on a level spot and pull them out so that the ends are about 8 or 9 feet across from each other. Push each one into the ground a little bit. Lean the other poles carefully in the forks, pushing each into the ground. Wrap the dangling ends of the rope around all the poles and tie another square knot. (You'll probably have to stand on a stool inside the poles or get an adult to help you do this.)

To put up the cover, tie the rope ends (of the rope holding the poles together) to the shower curtain hoop at the center of the cover. Use another square knot. Pull the teepee cover around the outside of the frame. Put rocks around the bottom to hold the cover in place, making sure it's taut. Fasten the front with safety pins, but leave a flap so you can get in and out. Put in a waterproof groundsheet.

Tie rope ends to shower curtain hoop.

REMEMBER: Your teepee will leak unless the cover material is waterproof.

Arrange the inside of your teepee the way the Indians did. Put a ring of stones in the center for the hearth, weapons such as bows and arrows near one side of the front flap, food and utensils on the other side, and a special rug or waterproof pillow on the far side opposite the flap for honored guests to sit on. It's easy to make drums (from coffee cans), feather headdresses (put feathers in a headband), and peace pipes (tape a stick to the bottom of a short section of a dried corncob).

P.S. To paint your face and body for a ceremonial dance, use powdered poster paint mixed with just a little water. Coat the area of skin you want to paint with a thin layer of petroleum jelly or cold cream before you paint it. Make sure you try painting just a small patch of skin at first to see if your skin is extra sensitive. Keep all paint away from your eyes and mouth.

Secret Hideouts

Three Camouflaged Hideouts for the Woods and Backyard

A camouflaged hideout should look as natural as possible. When people walk by, they won't even notice it—or you hiding inside.

Pine Tree Hideout

Prowl through the woods looking for a big pine tree with low branches that are nearly touching the ground. If you need to and you have permission, trim a few branches to make a space big enough for you and some gear and perhaps a friend and for an entrance. Gather extra pine boughs from the ground and lay them against the lower branches to fill in any open spots. Smooth out the ground under the tree, taking out

HINT: Cover the entrance with branches when you're not there.

any sticks or stones that won't be comfortable to sit on.

Crawl inside and lean more branches in front of the opening so they look like part of the tree. All people will see is a pine tree.

Runner Bean Secret Spot

This is the perfect camouflaged hideout for a back-yard gardener. By the middle of the summer, you'll be able to slide into it and be well hidden. You'll need six thin 6-foot-long poles, a ball of heavy twine, a packet of runner-bean seeds, and a dozen or so Baggie ties.

Tie three poles together about 1 foot from an end. Don't cut the twine. In a level sunny spot in your garden, stand the poles up and spread them out to make a tripod. Push the ends into the ground a little bit. Lean the other poles carefully in the forks, pushing their ends into the ground too. Then wrap twine around all the poles several times at the top and tie it tightly. Use a square knot (see page 6).

Plant hardy and fast-growing runner beans, such as scarlet runner, around the base. Follow the instructions on the packet. As the vines grow, train them up the poles, holding each vine in place with Baggie ties.

P.S. They have to be runner beans.

tie

baggie ties

39

Three-Bush Hideout

This is the very easiest camouflaged hideout to make, but you have to find three bushes—or evergreen trees—that are close together. Bushes with very leafy branches and cedar or hemlock trees are good choices. Squeeze into the center of the bushes or tree branches and remove a few branches to make a space for yourself. (You may not have to cut any branches, but if you do be sure you have permission.) Save the branches (or use any branches on the ground) to camouflage any opening you've made. Weave them in with the other branches once you're inside or fasten them with string.

How to Camouflage Yourself

The simplest way to camouflage yourself is just to wear clothes that are the same color as your surroundings. In the woods you'll be hard to see if you wear a shirt and pants that are a dull green and brown pattern—except in winter! You can also tape leaves to a brown or dark green shirt.

For a super camouflage outfit for the woods, add a special hat. Gather some very short, leafy branches and big leaves. Staple them to an old hat.

Secret Clubhouse

Most kids like to have a special meeting place for themselves and their friends where no adults or little brothers and sisters are allowed. This sturdy clubhouse is big enough for about five or six kids. It looks hard to build, but it's not. You can keep the inside of the clubhouse off-limits to nonmembers by putting in alarms and traps to help you catch any intruders.

This clubhouse is 5 feet long, 5 feet wide, and 5 feet high. If you want yours smaller or bigger, draw a plan first and figure out how long the boards should be.

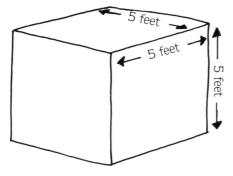

5 feet

5 feet

5 feet

P.S. Check with your parents to make sure the spot you've picked for the clubhouse is okay with them.

41

What You Need:

6   5-foot-long 2- × -4s
16   5-foot-long 1- × -4s
large pieces of plywood, scrap
    wood, or planks at least ½-inch
    thick for the floor, walls, and roof
2-inch- and 4-inch-long galvanized,
    coated nails
hammer
saw
tape measure

P.S. If you're not allowed to use a saw or don't know how, ask an adult for help.

What to Do:

1. Saw the planks and large pieces of wood in 5-foot-2-inch lengths.

2. Lay the 2-×-4s parallel and 10 inches apart on the ground where you want your clubhouse.

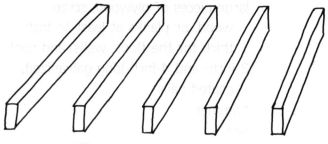

3. Keep the 2-×-4s parallel as you nail planks and large pieces of wood to them to make the floor. Nail a plank to each 2-×-4 it covers, using two nails.

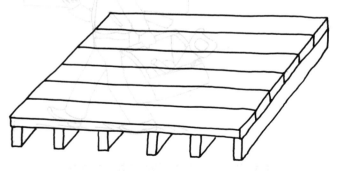

4. Make four wall frames by nailing the 1-×-4s like this.

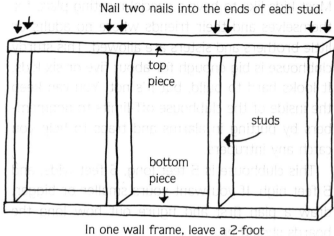

Nail two nails into the ends of each stud.

top piece

studs

bottom piece

In one wall frame, leave a 2-foot space for the door.

5. Nail big pieces of plywood or planks to the wall frames. Leave spaces for the entrance and windows, and for a secret door in back.

6. Put one wall frame on the floor and hold it in place. Drive the nails through the floor into the 2-×-4s. (You'll need a friend to help you do this.) After you nail the second wall frame to the floor, nail or screw the two wall frames together at the corner. Use the 2-inch nails. Keep going until all the frames are up.

7. Now nail plywood and planks across the tops of the wall frames to make a roof. You may need to use a ladder.

Inside, hang up an old shoe bag to hold secret messages and to store treasures.

Use crates for stools and a table. Tack pictures to the walls. Keep an old box with a padlock on it full of secret stuff. Write messages in secret code.

How to Tell If Anyone Has Invaded Your Space

• Sprinkle flour just inside the door when you leave. If anyone comes in, they'll leave footprints.
• Fasten the bottom of the door to the wall with a piece of adhesive tape. Someone trying to sneak in will pull it off the wall.
• Hang a bell inside the fabric door so it will ring if anyone comes in.

Nail up fabric to cover windows.

Nail up an old blanket to cover the doorway.

CLUB MEMBERS ONLY

NO LITTLE KIDS

Put up signs.

Treehouse Hideaway

A treehouse is the ultimate secret hideout because it's off the ground. That's why it's the best place to escape by yourself, to have a secret meeting of your friends when you don't want anyone to over-hear your plans, and to keep an eye on what's happening in your yard and neighborhood without being seen.

All treehouses have some kind of platform at-tached to trees or branches and some kind of ladder to get up to them—and down. But all tree-houses have to be different because the design depends on the size, shape, and number of trees you have.

P.S. Remember that a treehouse is a big project that takes time—a weekend or two—and probably adult help, especially when you're measuring and building the platform frame. And the best way to get adult help is to plan what you want to do first, gather the materials you can, and let the adults know in advance when you're going to need a hand.

Safety Steps before You Start

1. Choose a tree. Look for one with a thick trunk and at least two or three strong, spreading branches not too far off the ground. The branches will support your treehouse platform, so they need to be at least 8 inches thick. Your treehouse will be safer if you can reach the branches where you'll anchor your platform from the ground. *Don't* choose a tree near electric wires. If you can't find a tree that's the right shape, look for three trees that are close together.

The tree must be healthy and growing well. Do the branches have leaves or buds at their tips? Test their strength by swinging on them with a friend.

2. Clear the ground under the tree of all rocks, toys, branches, or anything else that would be dangerous to fall on.

3. Have your parents check on the tree you've chosen. Do they think it's safe to build in it? Is it okay with them if you use this particular tree? Driving nails into a tree may eventually weaken it.

4. Check at your city hall to find out whether your community has any building regulations that apply to treehouses. Some town building codes require nails of at least a certain size to be used, and specify how high a treehouse can be built.

Rules for Not Hurting the Tree or Trees

1. Build your treehouse in the spring or summer.
2. Don't strip off bark or chop into the tree.
3. Don't cut off large, live branches.
4. Use as few nails as possible, and don't pound many nails in one spot.

Designing

Look at your tree and plan where you're going to set the platform. You'll need to nail the platform frame (the floor) to at least three resting points. The platform also has to be as level as possible so it won't put more pressure on one branch than another. Here are three ways you might design your platform, depending on your tree's shape and whether you're using one tree or three.

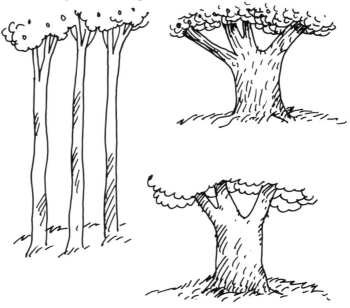

Building

You need these supplies:

> 3 or 4 blocks of wood (pieces of 2
> x 4 lumber about 12 inches long)
>
> 3 or 4 long pieces of 2 x 6 lumber
> (The length will depend on the
> size of the platform.)
>
> 10 or more long pieces of 2 x 4
> lumber
>
> lots of pieces of scrap board or ex-
> terior plywood at least ¾ inch
> thick
>
> a supply of 4-inch and about 10 6-
> inch galvanized coated nails
>
> an old straight ladder

You need these tools:

> level
>
> measuring stick
>
> saw
>
> hammer
>
> ladder

P.S. If you're using old pieces of lumber,
make sure no part of them is rotten or weak.

Here's what to do:

Step 1 Measure the distance between the resting
points.

Step 2 Saw the three pieces of 2 x 6 lumber to
the right lengths.

Step 3 Hold the long pieces in place (you'll need
help) to make sure the resting points you've picked
will work. You may have to adjust the shape of
the wood blocks by sawing off a corner or part
of it.

Step 4 Nail the blocks of wood to the resting
points. Use two or three nails to hold each one in
place. Space the nails out. After you nail the first
block, rest one end of a frame piece on it and hold
the other end up to the spot where you plan to
put the next block. Make sure the frame piece is
level _before_ nailing in that block. Do the same thing
with the third block.

HINT: The strongest way to nail the blocks
and frame is toenailing—driving the nail in
at an angle, like this:

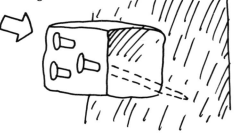

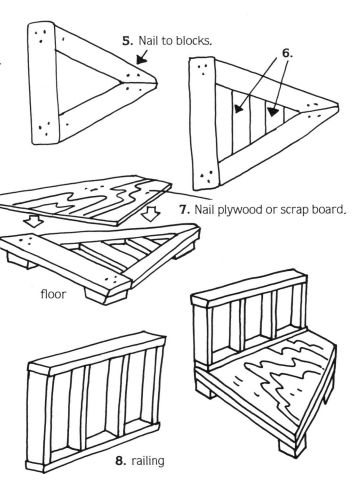

5. Nail to blocks.

6.

7. Nail plywood or scrap board.

floor

8. railing

Step 5 Nail one frame piece at a time to the top of the blocks. Use the 6-inch nails. You may have to trim the ends of the long piece so they're the right shape. Drive the nails into both the block and the tree at an angle.

Step 6 Nail several 2-x-4s inside the frame, like this, with no overlap. They should be 1 foot apart. You'll have to cut them to the right length first.

Step 7 Nail the pieces of scrap board or plywood across the frame boards to make a floor.

Step 8 Nail railings of 2-x-4s, like this, for wall frames. Be sure to leave an entrance that's at least 2 feet wide.

P.S. Never leave tools in the tree while you're working.

47

Step 9 Nail scrap board or plywood to the wall frames wherever you want walls. Leave spaces for windows and for the entrance.

Step 10 The easiest roof is a tarp draped over the top of the wall frames, or tied to tree branches above the platform.

Step 11 Now for the ladder. A rope ladder is one of the nicest ways to get in and out of the treehouse, but it's safer and more convenient to have a permanent ladder. Lean your old straight wooden ladder against the platform, at the entrance. Anchor it in the ground by digging holes and pushing the bottom ends of the ladder into them. Nail the other ends of the ladder to the platform frame. If you don't have a straight ladder, make one from 2-×-4s cut into pieces 18 inches long and two 2-×-6s, like this.

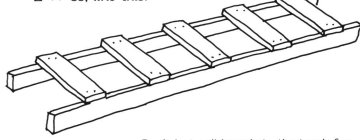

P.S. Don't just nail boards to the trunk for a ladder. It won't be safe.

48

Your treehouse is finished! Now just add a rope tied to a bucket or basket (that you can lower for supplies), a flag, and a few waterproof cushions for comfort. A whisk broom is handy for sweeping out leaves and dirt.

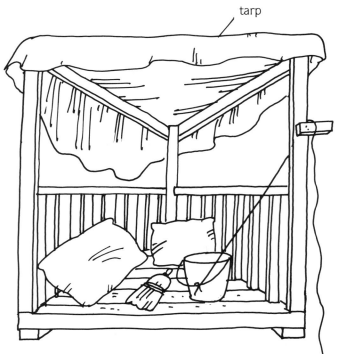

tarp

49

Outside Spaces

Two Snow Caves for an Arctic Trek

Eskimos build igloos from blocks of snow and ice when they are on hunting trips because those are the only materials around to use for building a shelter. When there's a big snowfall where you live, you can build one of these simple snow caves for your own Arctic trek. All you need is lots of snow that packs well and a few boards of wood, such as plywood sheets, wood planks, or an old wood door.

Snowball Cave

Stamp down a circle in the snow where you plan to build your cave. Roll lots of big snowballs and arrange them around the edge of the circle, leaving a space for a doorway. Pile another layer of snow-

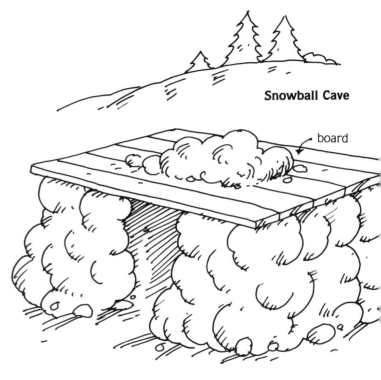

Snowball Cave

board

P.S. Using boards for the roof is important. A roof made of snow isn't safe.

P.S. When the snow starts to melt, check to make sure the boards won't fall.

Roll a few snowballs into the cave and mold them into seats and a table.

balls on top, and then another, and so on until your cave is as high as you want. Pack extra snow between the snowballs to make your walls smooth and solid.

Now put the boards across the top to make a roof. Pack some snow around them so they won't slide off. Don't heap snow on top.

51

Snow Mound Cave

You have to have a huge mound of snow that's partly packed down to make this cave. You can make a snow mound in your backyard by just piling up good packing snow until the pile is as high as you want your cave. (Make sure it is away from driveways or roads.) Flatten the top of the mound and put boards across for a roof. Hollow out a small cave under the boards. Leave the walls good and thick. Put a little snow on top of the boards for decoration. Double-check the roof when the snow cave begins to melt.

For a door to keep snowy winds out, nail an old blanket to one of the boards.

Or build a windbreak wall from snow in front of the cave opening.

Snow Mound Cave

For your Arctic trek, rig up a dogsled by hitching your dog (if he or she is big enough and willing) to a sled. Tie two ropes to the dog's collar and the front of the sled. Put your supplies in a plastic bag and tie them to the sled so they won't fall off, especially if Rex decides to bound off.

Take Thermoses of hot soup, hot cider, and hot cocoa, old blankets to sit on in your cave (an old fake-fur coat looks great), a flashlight, a small snow shovel, and a harpoon like this made from a long stick or piece of cardboard.

Wear warm clothing (it's important to keep your hands, head, and feet warm) and sunglasses or ski goggles so the glare of sun on the snow won't tire your eyes. Or make your own Eskimo snow goggles like these.

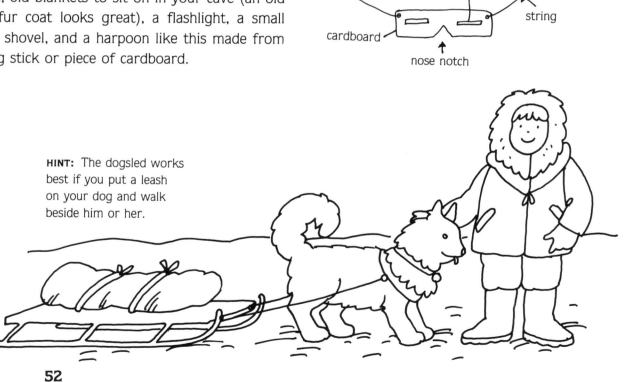

Make slits 1 ½ inches long and ⅛ inch high.

cardboard

string

nose notch

HINT: The dogsled works best if you put a leash on your dog and walk beside him or her.

Junkyard Fort

A junkyard fort can be used all year round. In the summer it's a good place for water wars with water-filled balloons, squirt guns, and hoses. In the winter, use it for snowball fights. In the spring and fall, it can be a western stockade, a medieval hilltop fort, or a futuristic space fort.

First collect some junk. Start at your town dump. If you live in a city, keep a lookout for junk left on the street for garbage collection. Are any buildings being renovated nearby? Check to see if old doors, window frames, paneling, and other stuff are being thrown out. Scrap-metal salvage yards, building contractors, electric power companies, and rug stores are other good places to ask for junk.

Keep stacking junk in your yard until you have enough. Then start attaching pieces together to make a big rectangle or circle. Wear your work gloves. You'll need a hammer, nails, wire cutters, pliers, and heavy wire.

> **WARNING:** Wear thick work gloves when handling junk. Watch out for broken glass and for nails or sharp bits of wood sticking out of things. Don't use these items or metal ones that are sharp or very rusty.

Junkyard Shopping List

wooden doors
big pieces of lumber
sheets of linoleum
window frames (Be sure there are
   no broken panes of glass.)
mattress springs
tables
table tops
beach umbrellas
boats
refrigerator doors
oil drums
sawhorses
tires
crates
concrete blocks
wooden barrels
furniture
heavy cardboard tubes
hubcaps
wooden telephone-wire spools
big plastic pipe
whatever else you can find

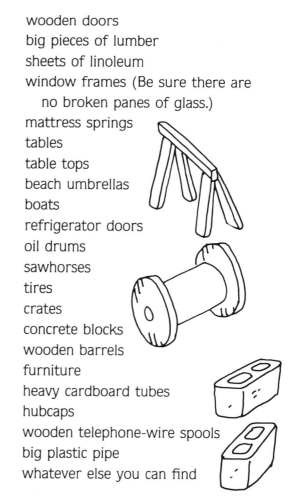

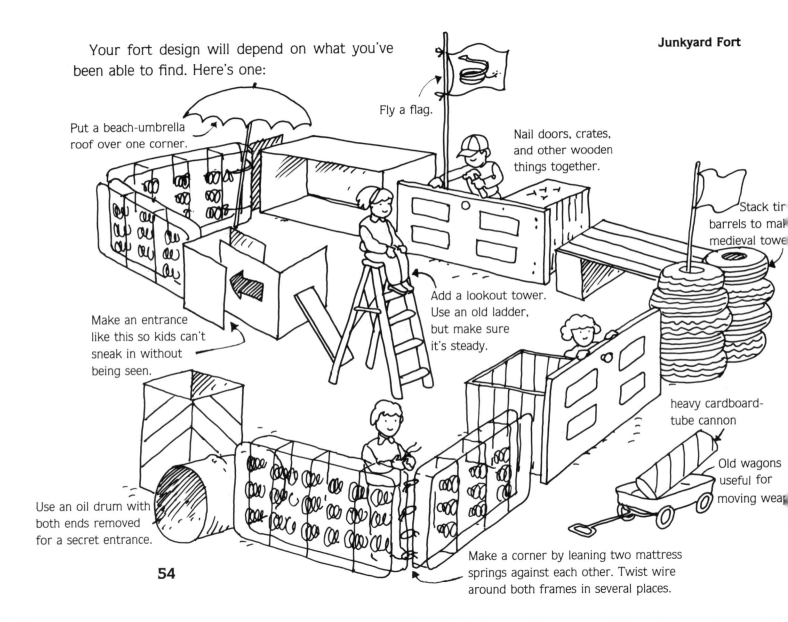

Your fort design will depend on what you've been able to find. Here's one:

Put a beach-umbrella roof over one corner.

Fly a flag.

Nail doors, crates, and other wooden things together.

Make an entrance like this so kids can't sneak in without being seen.

Add a lookout tower. Use an old ladder, but make sure it's steady.

Stack tir barrels to mal medieval towe

heavy cardboard-tube cannon

Old wagons useful for moving weap

Use an oil drum with both ends removed for a secret entrance.

Make a corner by leaning two mattress springs against each other. Twist wire around both frames in several places.

54

Now you're almost ready for a battle. Decide on the rules of warfare ahead of time. They should include:

NO USING DANGEROUS WEAPONS

NO THROWING ANYTHING AT OR HITTING ANYONE'S HEAD

In pretend battles nobody should get hurt.

If You Want to Be Knights
from the Middle Ages

Use hubcaps or garbage-can lids for shields, tie together the plastic circles that hold the tops of six-packs of cans to make chain-mail vests, and make cardboard swords from the sides of boxes. Wear an old football helmet covered with aluminum foil.

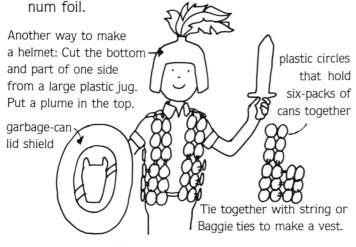

Another way to make a helmet: Cut the bottom and part of one side from a large plastic jug. Put a plume in the top.

garbage-can lid shield

plastic circles that hold six-packs of cans together

Tie together with string or Baggie ties to make a vest.

If You Want to Be Cowboys or Soldiers
Protecting a Western Stockade

Wear cowboy hats, neck scarves, vests, and cap pistols or squirt guns. Have a supply of play rifles (you can use broomsticks) and several cannons. Rig up a corral for the horses. Fly the American flag or make a flag with the insignia of a ranch such as ⌐⊐ for Lazy P Ranch or ★★★ for 3 Star Ranch.

If You Want to Be Superheroes
Defending a Space Fort

Make capes from large black and white plastic garbage bags. (CAUTION: Be sure not to put them over anyone's head and don't leave them around for little brothers and sisters to find.) Cover hard plastic dress-up hats with aluminum foil and attach pipe cleaners wherever you can to make antennas and wires. Wear boots and a fancy belt. Cover paper-towel tubes with aluminum foil to make ray guns.

HINT: Swordfight the way actors do in the movies. Take turns banging on each other's swords and shields.

Survival Lean-to

Suppose you were an explorer or trapper lost in the woods. What would you do? As long as you had a good knife, pieces of rope, and perhaps a small hatchet, you could build this emergency shelter with materials you found in the woods.

Before you start, measure your height and the length from your elbow to your fingertips. That way you'll be able to measure branches and trees without a ruler. Find two trees about 6 feet apart that have lower branches about 4 or 5 feet from the ground. (If you can't, get two thick branches of about equal length that look like this: ⫲
Pound them into the ground about 6 feet apart.)

Then look around for twelve fairly straight strong branches or saplings that are at least 7 feet long and six shorter ones to use as poles. You'll also need three pieces of rope: one 12 feet long and two each 10 feet long. If possible, cut the branches from a fallen tree (but not one that has rotted), or use branches that are lying on the ground. Check to see whether anyone in the neighborhood is cutting down a tree. That might supply most of what you need. (Make sure you get permission to cut branches or trees.)

WARNING: If you're not allowed to use knives or don't know how to cut and trim branches, ask an adult to help you.

Trim off small branches, leaving nubs of smaller offshoots, like these:

Save the branches if they have thick, leafy foliage or are evergreens with thickly clustered needles, like balsam or hemlock. Gather more evergreen boughs or leafy branches to add to your pile.

HINT: The open side of the shelter should face away from the wind.

Now follow these steps.

1. Place the thickest long pole on two branches of the two trees to make a ridgepole.

2. With your knife, sharpen seven of the long poles at one end. Lean these, pointed edge down, against the ridgepole about 8 inches apart. Brace the end poles against the tree trunks. Push the sharpened ends into the ground a little bit.

3. Wrap one end of a 12-foot-long piece of rope twice around one tree. Then lash the leaning poles to the ridgepole the way the picture shows. Wrap the other end of the rope around the other tree.

4. Place the remaining long poles across the leaning poles to make a lattice. If they bend enough, weave them over and under the leaning poles. If not, rest them in nubs where possible and lash them to the two leaning end poles just the way you lashed the leaning poles to the ridgepole. Use two pieces of rope about 10 feet long.

5. Sharpen the shorter poles at one end. Push them into the ground to make the sides of your lean-to as in the picture.

6. Start hanging the evergreen or leafy branches on the frame. Begin at the back of the lean-to, weaving them in and out one row at a time. Overlap the rows to make your roof thick and waterproof. Weave more branches into the sides.

7. Cover the floor with the tips of evergreen branches, pine needles, or grass.

This shelter takes time to build, but it will usually last a few months. If you make the roof thick enough, it will keep rain out. Repairing a leaky roof is easy—add a few more branches.

Survival Lean-to

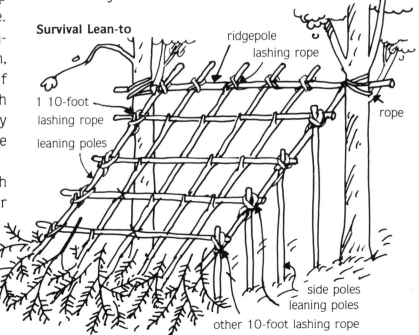

ridgepole

lashing rope

1 10-foot lashing rope

leaning poles

rope

side poles

leaning poles

other 10-foot lashing rope

Survival Gear and Techniques

The Essential Survival Kit

Careful campers, hikers, and explorers take along a kit of small items to help them survive in an emergency. A large-sized metal bandage tin with a flip top or a waterproof plastic zip bag makes a good container. Put in

a coiled-up fishing line, a hook, and several sinkers

survival food (beef jerky, chocolate bar, fruit-and-nut pemmican)

matches in waterproof container (You can waterproof wooden strike-anywhere kitchen matches by dipping the tips in melted candle wax or nail polish.)

first-aid supplies (Band-Aids, small roll of adhesive tape, gauze pads, antiseptic, tweezers)

snakebite kit

flashlight

compass

insect repellent

map

small mirror for signaling for help

You should also carry extra clothing, a canteen of water, a coil of nylon rope, your knife, and, if you have one, a small spade in a backpack.

WARNING: <u>Don't</u> drink water from any pond, stream, or lake. Bring your own.

Signal for Help

- With a mirror: Face the sun and catch the sunlight on the mirror. Hold it steady while you cover and uncover it with your hand to make flashes. Three rapid flashes is the usual call for help.
- With a fire: When your fire is burning well, throw on some damp wood and leaves to create a column of smoke.

Make a Simple Fishing Pole

Cut a thin, green (springy and living) branch or sapling about 4 feet long. Try bending it—the thinner end should be very flexible. Wind the fishing line around the tip of the pole and tape it carefully with adhesive tape. Tie one or two sinkers 2 feet above the end of the line and then tie on the hook (use square knots—see page 6). Dig up some worms for bait or use insects or a bit of your food.

tape

Build a Fire

<u>Always</u> ask an adult's permission before starting a fire. Also find out what the local fire laws are.

For the safest fire, first make a circle of stones. Gather tinder (dry grass, birch bark, dead twigs and evergreen needles), lots of kindling (twigs and small sticks from dead, dry branches), and a few small dry logs.

Lay two thick sticks in your circle as shown and put tinder between them. Place another stick across the two sticks. Lean pieces of kindling against the top stick, over the tinder. Light the tinder with your match.

When the fire gets going, add larger pieces of wood in a criss-cross pattern.

Follow these campfire safety rules:

1. Build your fire away from trees, stumps, or brush. Clear a 3-foot area around it.

2. Have a pile or bucket of dirt or sand or a bucket of water handy BEFORE you build the fire.

3. Don't leave a fire burning if you go off for a hike. Cover it with dirt or sand or pour water on it. Make sure it is COMPLETELY OUT. There should be no smoke or smoldering pieces of wood.

1. circle of stones

2. small logs and tinder

3. crisscross logs

sand or dirt

4.

Empty Lot Obstacle Course

Here's a way to liven up a lazy afternoon. Get together with some friends and canvass the neighborhood for junk you can use to set up an obstacle course in a nearby empty lot—or someone's big backyard. Planks, tires of different sizes, sawhorses, ladders, ropes, crates, oil drums, barrels, cardboard cartons, and a small plastic wading pool are some items to scrounge. Check over everything carefully. Don't use anything that has sharp parts sticking out (including broken glass) or that tips over easily.

Your course will depend on what you've collected, what's already in the empty lot (there might be trees, some concrete pipe, stumps, a mud hill, and so on), the kinds of activities you and your friends want to include, and the season of the year. Set up your course so kids have to do a lot of different things—running, jumping, hopping, climbing, crawling, swinging, balancing, throwing, sliding. Every so often kids should have to stop and perform a task, such as doing a handstand or climbing a tree and bringing down two leaves.

Here are some ideas:

Empty Lot Obstacle Course

stepladder with bell
Climb up and
ring bell.

START

1-inch hemp or sisal
rope; tie simple knots
in it (see page 6) and
attach to branch
with two half-hitch
knots (see page 7).
Swing over the pool.

sawhorse
Go under.

concrete
blocks
Hop on
and off.

oil drum
Crawl through.

spool table
Climb over.

Have everyone walk through the whole course at least once to become familiar with it. Then start some races. Time each person from start to finish with a stopwatch or kitchen timer to see who is the fastest. Or divide the group into teams and see which team is the fastest. Deduct a certain number of seconds for a penalty if someone skips a part of the course. When everyone is ready for something new, just change the course!

P.S. Adapt to the season. In the summer, have a water slide at the finish line. In the winter, make tunnels and high jumps from snow.

tires of
different sizes
Jump in and out.

Walk the plank.

broomstick
on 2 sawhorses
or crates for
high jump
Jump over.

large concrete pipe
Shinny along.

FINISH

Practical and Portable Playhouses

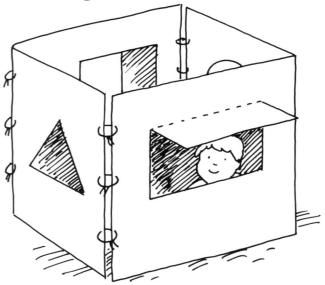

Two Practically Instant Portable Playhouses

How about a playhouse whose shape you can change whenever you want? You can store both of these playhouses under your bed and add more parts when you need them.

Look for strong appliance cartons and the kind of carton large pieces of furniture come in. Cardboard that is double thick is the best.

Cut panels from the sides of the cartons with a mat knife and ruler. (Page 5 tells how to cut cardboard safely and well.) Leave some of them solid, and cut windows and doors of different shapes and sizes in the others, like this:

The Baggie Tie and Panel Playhouse

For this playhouse, collect lots of long Baggie ties, the kind with wire inside that come in boxes of plastic garbage bags. Choose panels that are all about the same height. Punch holes along two opposite edges of each panel with a sharp nail. Make the holes at least $1/2$ inch from the edge, and make at least one hole every foot or so.

Join two panels together by pushing one Baggie tie through holes in both and twisting the ends together. Press the ends flat so there's nothing sharp sticking out.

Keep joining panels together until your playhouse is as big as you want. Decorate the panels with markers or paint, or glue on cloth and paper.

HINT: Cut as you collect so you can store the panels until you have enough. Then decide which playhouse you want to make.

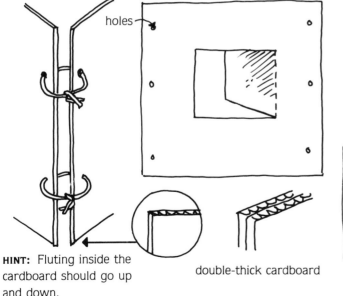

holes

HINT: Fluting inside the cardboard should go up and down.

double-thick cardboard

The Slot Playhouse

Panels for this playhouse can be different widths, but it works best if they are all the same height. With a mat knife, cut two slots in opposite ends of each panel. They should be about $1/4$ to $1/2$ inch wide and about 2 inches from the panel edges. Make them half the height of the panel. Cut an additional slot in the center of a few panels.

Decorate the panels with paint, markers, or glue and cloth. Keep paint and glue away from the slots.

When the panels are dry, slide one slot into another. Keep joining panels until your playhouse is the size and shape you want.

The Slot Playhouse

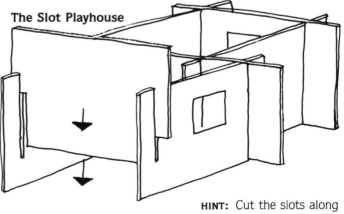

HINT: Cut the slots along the fluting, not across it.

A Cardboard Carton Stage

This stage is sure to help make your next play a hit. It's big enough for several characters to be onstage at once. Two back entrances make it easy for characters to get on and off stage without being seen—just the way they do in a real theater. It won't take you long to build it, and after the play is over, you can roll up the scenery backdrops and curtains and store them right in the stage boxes.

Here's what to do.

Get two large refrigerator cartons. When you get them home, stand them opposite each other wherever you plan to have your play, with the opened ends up. Cut the two facing panels on three

sides with a mat knife or bread knife (read how to cut cardboard on page 5) to make two doors. Pull open the doors. (You're going to use these panels for part of the backdrop where you attach the scenery.)

Cut backstage openings in the back panels of the two cartons. Leave at least a few inches of cardboard on the sides and at the top to keep the stage stable. Use silver duct tape to attach the two extra cardboard pieces to the two open doors to make the backdrop about 6 feet wide.

Now paint the outside of the theater. Use your imagination.

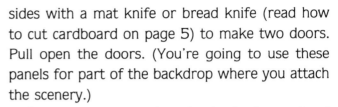

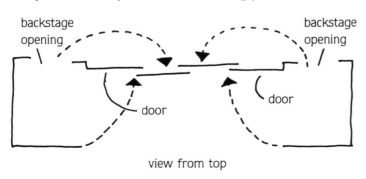

view from top

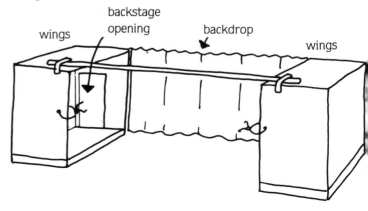

Hanging the stage curtain is next. Ask your mother for a curtain rod that extends to 7½ or 8 feet (or you could buy one at a hardware store) and two old twin-bed-sized sheets (or old curtains or pieces of fabric as long as the height of the boxes). Cut a hole at each end of the hem in both sheets. Slide the sheets onto the curtain rod and push them to the middle. Rest the two ends of the rod on top of the boxes, an inch or so from the edge. Tape the rod in place securely with silver duct tape. Practice opening and closing the curtains to make sure the rod is in the right place. Your theater is ready to go!

Now for the scenery. Paint the scenes for your play on big sheets of newsprint drawing paper. Hang them from the backdrop with spring-loaded clothespins or tape them in place with masking tape.

What other scenery will you need? Make a list of items, such as a table and chairs, a ladder, a tree, plants, and so on. You can make some of these out of cardboard—like the table, throne, or tree shown below.

Make a list of characters and the costumes they'll wear. Hang hats, wigs, and costumes on hooks in the wings.

flat sheet of cardboard

box

cardboard table

big box

small box

cardboard throne

cardboard tree

Two Terrific Puppet Theaters

Do you like to put on puppet shows for friends and brothers and sisters? If you do, you need some kind of puppet theater where you (the puppeteer) can hide while you're making your puppets talk.

Portable Doorway Puppet Theater

You don't want to buy anything if you don't have to, so ask your parents whether they have a tension rod you could have. If they don't, buy one from a hardware store. It will cost about two or three dollars. Measure the width of the doorway that you plan to use for this theater so you'll know what size to buy. The 28-inch-to-48-inch size is probably your best bet because most doorways are about 30 inches wide. Buy the skinny $^{7}/_{16}$-inch rod.

Next you need a piece of heavy dark cloth that's at least the same width as your door and about 4 feet long. Felt is especially good, but any kind of fabric will do. (Your parents may have some old drapes you can use.)

Fold over one end of the fabric about an inch

and a half. Staple or sew along the edge to make a hem for the curtain rod. Fix the curtain rod according to the directions that come with it, then slide the rod into the hem. Before you put the whole thing up, think about where the rod should be. Lightly mark the doorway with pencil and then put up the rod. Make a hem in the fabric so it just touches the floor. Staple or glue on cut-out felt shapes, lace, or ribbon.

Refrigerator Carton Puppet Theater

Stand the refrigerator carton so the unopened reinforced end is on the floor. Read about how to cut cardboard on page 5. Then cut a door opening in the back panel for the puppeteers. Leave at least a few inches of cardboard on each side and at the top. (This helps keep the theater stable.)

To figure out where to cut the stage opening in the opposite side, stand or sit in front of the carton and hold up your hand as you would to move a puppet in a show. Then you'll be able to tell how high the opening should be. Mark lines for it.

Cut the horizontal top and bottom lines first. Then cut a vertical line between them to make two flaps. Climb inside. Run the mat knife lightly down the two uncut sides and bend the flaps out carefully. (This helps the flaps open and close easily.)

Cut off the top flaps from the front and side. Tape the back flap or a piece of cardboard across the top of the box at the rear to form a partial ceiling. (You need this so you can hang your background from it.) Use strong duct tape or wide masking tape.

That's all. You're ready to decorate your theater with paint or by gluing pictures or paper shapes or glitter, or all of them, on it.

To Make a Background

Cut the extra cardboard piece (or a big piece of lighter-weight cardboard) wider than the stage opening and long enough to hang from the top of the box. Tape it to the edge of the back flap at the top of the box with strong duct tape. Paint your backgrounds or glue pictures on paper and tape the scenes to the cardboard piece.

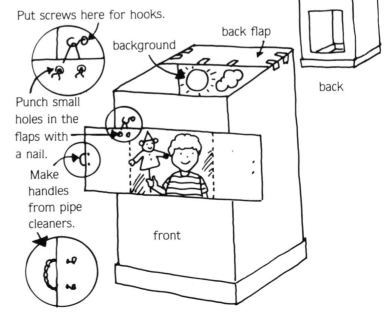

Put screws here for hooks.

background

back flap

back

Punch small holes in the flaps with a nail.

Make handles from pipe cleaners.

front

How to Set Up the Puppet Show

You have to have puppets, of course. And you also need an idea for a puppet play. You could write an outer-space story or a silly-people play yourself or you could make a play from a folktale or story that you know. Here are three types of puppets that you can make into whatever characters you want.

Sock Puppet

Gather some old clean socks, white glue, scissors, tape, buttons, colored paper, yarn, string, and pipe cleaners. If you want to make a more complicated puppet, you may need a needle and thread.

Quick Stick Puppet

Draw your character on cardboard and cut it out with scissors. Paint and decorate it. Tape it to a narrow piece of strong cardboard about 1 to 2 feet long or to a stick that length.

P.S. When your puppets are ready and your play is written, practice your show a few times before you invite a crowd to see it.

70

Glue or sew on: eyes nose mouth

Tape on: a hat hair antlers or antennas ears whiskers

Sock Puppet

Cut holes for your little finger and thumb and sew on 2 fingers cut from an old glove.

Tie the toe of the sock to make a nose.

Stick Puppet

Balloon and Papier-Mâché Puppet

This kind of puppet is big and impressive-looking and a lot of fun to make, but it takes time. For each one you need a balloon and a paper-towel or toilet-paper tube. You also need newspaper, white glue and liquid starch, and a shallow container for the glue mixture.

Mix 1 cup white glue with 1 quart liquid starch and pour some in the container. Blow up the balloon and tie the end. Tear the newspaper into strips about 1/2 inch wide and 6 inches long. Dip them into the glue mixture, pulling off the extra glue with your fingers. Then smooth each strip onto the balloon. Make sure you put them on in all directions so your puppet head will be strong. After you have put on three layers of strips, let them dry thoroughly. This may take a day or so.

After it is dry, add a paper-towel-tube neck and other features, attaching them with strips of newspaper dipped in the glue mixture, and an extra layer or two of strips. Let it dry thoroughly again. Then paint and decorate. Make a costume and tape it to the paper-towel tube, like this.

71

HINT: Set your balloon on a tin can or cottage cheese container base while you're working.

tin can

Balloon and Papier-Mâché Puppet

paper towel tube

The Basic Store

Once you have this basic store set up, you're almost ready for business. You can turn it into a bakery, or a lemonade stand, or a craft shop, or even a post office where all your friends in the neighborhood can send messages to one another. The kind of shop you make it into will depend on what you feel like selling.

To start, you need:

> 4 large cardboard cartons (about 2 feet high) or 4 orange crates, all the same size, for the display shelves
>
> 1 long, wide piece of wood or strong cardboard (1 panel from a refrigerator carton will work well) for a counter
>
> extra pieces of cardboard
>
> silver duct tape or white glue or carpenter's glue
>
> 2 straight sticks about 2 feet long

If you have cartons, you'll have to make shelves for them from the extra pieces of cardboard before you set up the store. Here's how. Cut four pieces of cardboard, one for each box, about the same width as a box but 12 inches longer. (See page 5 for how to cut cardboard easily.) Fold down about 6 inches on each side and lightly run a mat knife along the two folds.

Slide each shelf into a box. Tape the two folded edges to the box, or put plenty of glue on the folded edges and then place each shelf in a box.

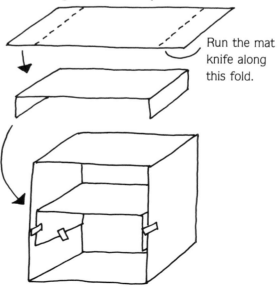

Run the mat knife along this fold.

Next, put two cartons a few feet apart and lay the long piece of cardboard or wood across them. Set the other two cartons on the ends. Now you've got your basic store.

(If you were lucky enough to find orange crates, you can figure out what to do.)

You need a sign for your store, so decide what kind it will be. Cut a long, narrow piece of cardboard for your store sign. Paint the store name on it. When it's dry, tape it to the two sticks and tape the two sticks to the two top cartons.

Basic Store Equipment and Supplies

　　　　a toy cash register or money box on
　　　　　　the counter
　　　　money
　　　　merchandise

To make a money box, glue or tape pieces of cardboard to divide a shallow box.

To make play money, cut and color pieces of paper for dollars. Cut circles of different sizes for pennies, dimes, nickels, and quarters. Cover them with aluminum foil.

Of course, you'll want to stock your shelves with products or merchandise for your customers to buy.

How to Turn Your Basic Store into a Basement Bakery

A playdough bakery is a good project for several kids on a rainy afternoon.

You need the basic store, plus a baker's apron and hat, a bowl and measuring cups, a scale (for weighing cookies), shopping bags and cake boxes, and plates, trays, and baskets for displaying your playdough breads and pastries. Small squares of paper make fine price tags.

So start baking. Here's an easy recipe for a big batch of playdough:

4 cups flour
2 cups salt
1 $1/3$ cups water
food coloring (if you want to make colored playdough)

Mix the flour and salt together. Then add the water, a little at a time, squeezing and kneading until the dough is smooth. (Add the food coloring to the water <u>before</u> you mix it in if you want colored playdough. Use several drops.)

Shape the playdough into bread, cookie, cake, biscuit, and roll shapes.

Decorate with glitter, seeds and beans, or salt (it will make playdough items shiny). Bake your playdough shapes in the oven at 225°. Bake small, thin cookies for about 10 to 15 minutes on each side. Bake thick items 1 to 1½ hours on each side.

When they are cool, paint your baked goods or color them with felt-tip markers.

Arrange them in your bakery and attach the price tags. Take turns buying and selling.

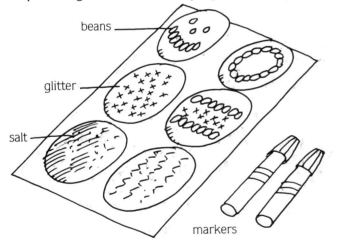

REMINDER: Check with an adult before using the oven.

HINT: When the paint dries, put on two coats of clear nail polish if you want them to last.

Make a Craft Shop

To change your bakery into a craft shop, just make bracelets, bead and pendant necklaces, tiles, ornaments, and small animal statues from playdough. This is a good type of store for a street or school fair.

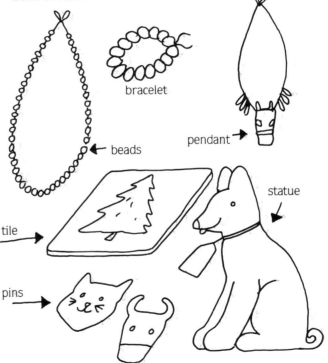

How to Turn Your Basic Store into an Old-Fashioned Lemonade Stand

Wait for a hot day. That's when people really want something cold to drink and when your lemonade stand can make money.

Besides the basic store, you'll need Thermos jugs, paper cups, a measuring cup, cardboard for extra signs, masking tape, a box or garbage can for cups people throw away, and real money for change. You'll also need lemonade, of course.

Now for the lemonade. The very best kind is made from real lemons, sugar, and water. Cut ten big lemons in half and squeeze out all the juice. Pour it into a juice jar (that has a lid) and add 1 1/2 cups sugar. Stir and then shake until the sugar dissolves. Pour the mixture into a 1-gallon Thermos jug, and add two trays of ice cubes and 10 cups of cold water. (Use a big bowl or jug for mixing if you have only small Thermoses. After the lemonade is mixed, pour it into the small Thermoses.) Stir and taste. Put the lemonade in the refrigerator while you set up the stand.

P.S. Keep track of all the money you spend for cups, lemons, etc., so you'll know how much to charge.

76

Turn the boxes so the shelves face each other. Keep your cups on the shelves. Put up a sign with the price—30¢ is about right for real lemonade. Now get your lemonade jug and you're in business. Keep your trash container under the counter.

HINT: The best spot for selling anything is wherever there are a lot of people. So pick a busy sidewalk spot, preferably a shady one. Put an extra sign at the nearest corner so people will be looking for your stand and thinking about your lemonade.